ADDRESSES

CHRONICLE BOOKS

Design by Chip Kidd and Chin-Yee Lai
Cover design by Henry Quiroga
Photographs by Geoff Spear

Manufactured in China

Chronicle Books LLC
85 Second Street, San Francisco, CA 94105
www.chroniclebooks.com

ISBN: 0-8118-2903-0

Distributed in Canada by Raincoast Books
9050 Shaughnessy Street, Vancouver, B.C.
V6P 6E5

10 9 8 7 6 5 4 3 2

YOU AND I.. KING AND QUEEN OF CRIME! ... WE'D MAKE A GREAT TEAM! WITH YOU AS MY PARTNER WE...
SORRY, YOUR PROPOSITION TEMPTS ME BUT WE WORK ON DIFFERENT SIDES OF THE LAW!.. LET'S GO

PUT HIS COSTUME BACK ON HIM SO IT WILL NEVER BE FOUND EITHER! I TOOK EVERYTHING OUT OF THE UTILITY BELT!
THAT'S A CLEVER IDEA, CATWOMAN. DO IT, BOYS! WE MUST DESTROY AL THE EVIDENCE THAT COULD PROVE WE MURDERED HIM!

SO BATMAN TRAILED ME! WELL, HE'LL LEARN THAT THOSE WHO BOTHER CATS CAN GET SCRATCHED!
CLAW RETRACTOR

CAGED BY
THE CAT-WOMAN

PQ

TOLL OF
TORTURE

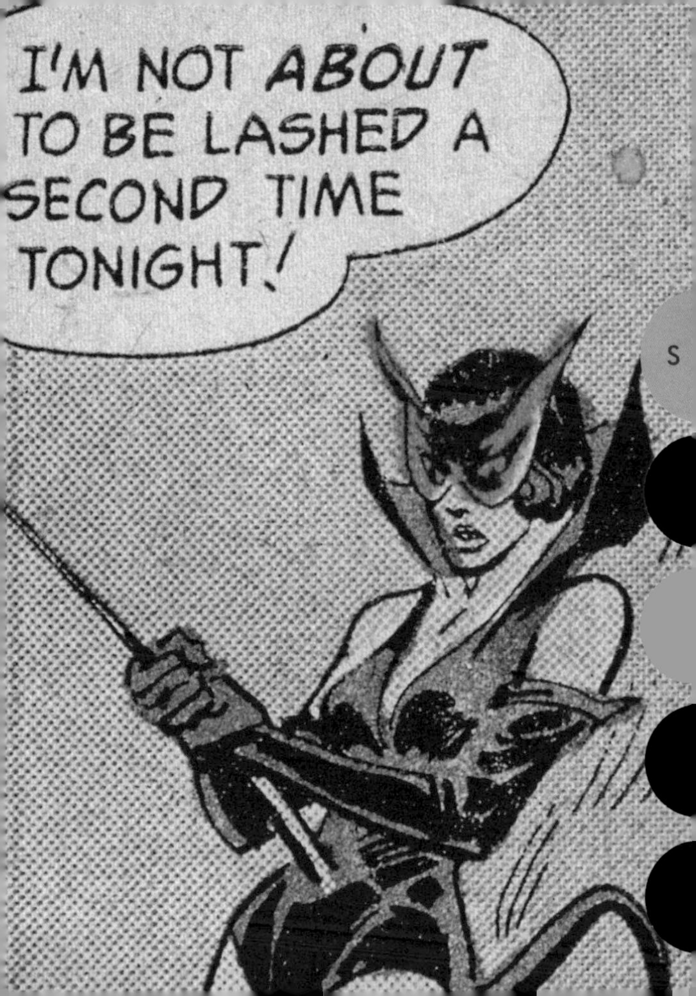
I'M NOT ABOUT TO BE LASHED A SECOND TIME TONIGHT!

15

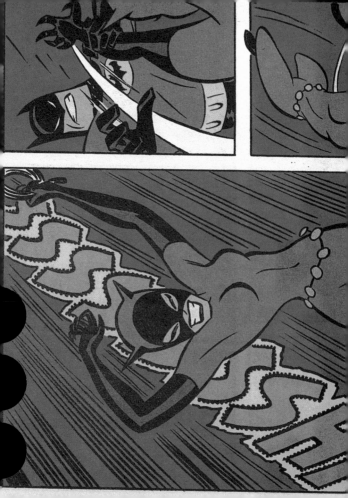

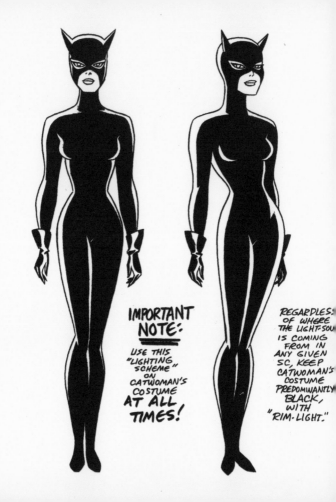

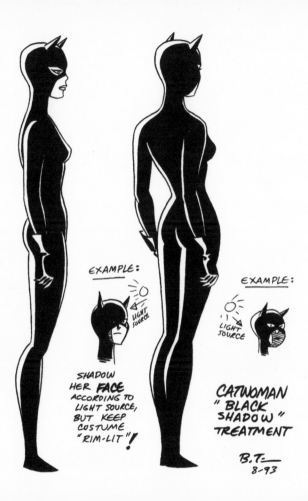

EXAMPLE:

LIGHT SOURCE

SHADOW HER **FACE** ACCORDING TO LIGHT SOURCE, BUT KEEP COSTUME "RIM-LIT"!

EXAMPLE:

LIGHT SOURCE

CATWOMAN "BLACK SHADOW" TREATMENT

B.T.
8-93